D1525680

WITHDRAWN

FLORIDA

A MyReportLinks.com Book

Stephen Feinstein

MyReportLinks.com Books

an imprint of

 Enslow Publishers, Inc.

Box 398, 40 Industrial Road

Berkeley Heights, NJ 07922

USA

MyReportLinks.com Books, an imprint of Enslow Publishers, Inc. MyReportLinks is a trademark of Enslow Publishers, Inc.

Copyright © 2003 by Enslow Publishers, Inc.

Library of Congress Cataloging-in-Publication Data

Feinstein, Stephen.
  Florida / Stephen Feinstein.
    p. cm. — (States)
Summary: Discusses the land and climate, economy, government, and history of the state with a higher percentage of retirees than any other. Includes Internet links to Web sites, source documents, and photographs related to Florida.
Includes bibliographical references and index.
  ISBN 0-7660-5027-0
  1. Florida—Juvenile literature. [1. Florida.] I. Title. II. States (Series : Berkeley Heights, N.J.)
  F311.3 .F45 2002
  975.9—dc21
                        2002008694

Printed in the United States of America

10 9 8 7 6 5 4 3 2 1

To Our Readers:
Through the purchase of this book, you and your library gain access to the Report Links that specifically back up this book.

The Publisher will provide access to the Report Links that back up this book and will keep these Report Links up to date on **www.myreportlinks.com** for three years from the book's first publication date.

We have done our best to make sure all Internet addresses in this book were active and appropriate when we went to press. However, the author and the Publisher have no control over, and assume no liability for, the material available on those Internet sites or on other Web sites they may link to.

The usage of the MyReportLinks.com Books Web site is subject to the terms and conditions stated on the Usage Policy Statement on **www.myreportlinks.com**.

In the future, a password may be required to access the Report Links that back up this book. The password is found on the bottom of page 4 of this book.

Any comments or suggestions can be sent by e-mail to comments@myreportlinks.com or to the address on the back cover.

Photo Credits: © 1995 PhotoDisc, Inc., pp. 12, 25, 42, 45; © 1998 Corbis Corporation, p. 13; © Corel Corporation, pp. 3, 10, 19, 23, 43; Archaeology, Inc., p. 34; Enslow Publishers, Inc., pp. 1, 17; Florida Citrus, p. 27; Florida Department of State, pp. 10, 31, 37; Jay I. Kislak Foundation, p. 33; MyReportLinks.com Books, p. 4; National Wildlife Federation, p. 20; Online Sunshine for Kids, pp. 29, 30; PBS, p. 40; Smithsonian Institution, p. 38; Voice From the Gaps, p. 15.

Cover Photo: © 1995 PhotoDisc, Inc.

Cover Description: Aerial view of Miami Beach.

Contents

MyReportLinks.com Books
Great Books, Great Links, Great for Research!

MyReportLinks.com Books present the information you need to learn about your report subject. In addition, they show you where to go on the Internet for more information. The pre-evaluated Report Links that back up this book are kept up to date on **www.myreportlinks.com**. With the purchase of a MyReportLinks.com Books title, you and your library gain access to the Report Links that specifically back up that book. The Report Links save hours of research time and link to dozens—even hundreds—of Web sites, source documents, and photos related to your report topic.

Please see "To Our Readers" on the Copyright page for important information about this book, the MyReportLinks.com Books Web site, and the Report Links that back up this book.

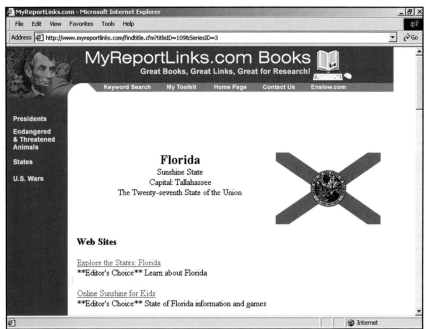

Access:

The Publisher will provide access to the Report Links that back up this book and will try to keep these Report Links up to date on our Web site for three years from the book's first publication date. Please enter **SFL2802** if asked for a password.

Report Links

The Internet sites described below can be accessed at
http://www.myreportlinks.com

▶**Explore the States: Florida**   *EDITOR'S CHOICE

America's Story from America's Library, a Library of Congress Web site, explores the state of Florida. Here you will learn about Florida's history and find links to interesting stories about the Sunshine State.

Link to this Internet site from http://www.myreportlinks.com

▶**Online Sunshine for Kids**   *EDITOR'S CHOICE

This site, from the Florida State Legislature, contains information about Florida's government. An online tour of the state capitol and games and puzzles having to do with state government are featured.

Link to this Internet site from http://www.myreportlinks.com

▶**Florida Facts**   *EDITOR'S CHOICE

This Web site from the Florida Department of State, Division of Historical Resources, contains state facts, state symbols, and Florida history, including the history of Seminole Indians in Florida and the state's part in the Civil War.

Link to this Internet site from http://www.myreportlinks.com

▶**Florida Then and Now**   *EDITOR'S CHOICE

This Web site features some biographies of famous Floridians, articles about historical events, descriptions of native peoples, and other resources.

Link to this Internet site from http://www.myreportlinks.com

▶**Myths and Dreams: Exploring the Cultural Legacies of Florida and the Caribbean**   *EDITOR'S CHOICE

This site contains articles about Florida's culture and history, including African Americans in Florida and profiles of important Floridians such as Zora Neale Hurston and David Levy Yulee.

Link to this Internet site from http://www.myreportlinks.com

▶**The American Experience—Mr. Miami Beach**   *EDITOR'S CHOICE

At this PBS Web site you will find the story of Carl Fischer, known as Mr. Miami Beach because he transformed what was once swampland into a prime vacation spot.

Link to this Internet site from http://www.myreportlinks.com

 The Internet sites described below can be accessed at
http://www.myreportlinks.com

▶ **The Adams-Onís Treaty**
Here you will find the complete text of the Adams-Onís Treaty in which
Spain ceded Florida to the United States. Historical notes on the treaty
are included.

Link to this Internet site from http://www.myreportlinks.com

▶ **American Masters—Tennessee Williams**
American playwright Tennessee Williams lived in Key West for more than
thirty years. His life and work are profiled here. A video clip of a film adapted
from one of Williams's plays is also featured.

Link to this Internet site from http://www.myreportlinks.com

▶ **Dalí Museum**
Visit the Salvador Dalí Museum in St. Petersburg, Florida. Here you will find
descriptions of the artist's different periods of work, biographical information,
a history of the museum, visitor information, and many of Dalí's paintings.

Link to this Internet site from http://www.myreportlinks.com

▶ **Election 2000**
This site examines the results of the 2000 presidential election, which
Florida voters played a pivotal role in. Included are statistics, speeches,
articles, and videos.

Link to this Internet site from http://www.myreportlinks.com

▶ **Endangered Species in the Everglades**
This National Wildlife Federation site profiles the endangered species of
the Florida Everglades, including the American alligator, Florida panther,
and the green turtle. Habitat, population, and human and animal behavior
are examined.

Link to this Internet site from http://www.myreportlinks.com

▶ **Ernest Hemingway Home and Museum**
At the official site of the Ernest Hemingway Home and Museum you will
learn about Hemingway's Key West years, his cats, the books he wrote there,
and the museum itself.

Link to this Internet site from http://www.myreportlinks.com

Report Links

The Internet sites described below can be accessed at
http://www.myreportlinks.com

▶ **Florida Civic Ed: Florida Constitution**
Florida's unique constitutional system is profiled in this site, and a
history of the Florida constitution is provided. A video tour shows
Florida's democracy in action.

Link to this Internet site from http://www.myreportlinks.com

▶ **Florida Historical Contexts**
This Web site explores the history of Paleo-Indians in Florida. Here
you will learn about the objects they used, the environments they lived
in, and their culture.

Link to this Internet site from http://www.myreportlinks.com

▶ **Florida Museum of Natural History**
At the Florida Museum of Natural History site you can take a virtual
tour of St. Augustine and visit the Hall of Florida Fossils. You can also
explore the photo gallery and learn about the museum's holdings.

Link to this Internet site from http://www.myreportlinks.com

▶ **Florida: Sunshine State**
This Web site provides a quick list of facts and figures about Florida,
with links to weather information, historical information, maps, and
much more.

Link to this Internet site from http://www.myreportlinks.com

▶ **Kennedy Space Center Home Page**
Learn about Cape Canaveral and NASA history at the official site
of the Kennedy Space Center. You can also visit the interactive
"Fun Space" for launch simulation and take a virtual tour of the
space shuttle.

Link to this Internet site from http://www.myreportlinks.com

▶ **Keys Historeum**
The Historical Preservation Society of the Upper Keys site includes a
history of the Florida Keys, important events, dates, and people.

Link to this Internet site from http://www.myreportlinks.com

Report Links

The Internet sites described below can be accessed at
http://www.myreportlinks.com

▶**Miami Beach**
At PBS's "Going Places" Web site you can learn all about Miami. Here you will find a slide show, an insider's guide, and a clickable map with links to articles about notable Miami sites.

Link to this Internet site from http://www.myreportlinks.com

▶**Miami Deco**
Here you will learn about Miami's Art Deco district, known as South Beach, and view its buildings while learning about its history. A glossary of Art Deco terms is included.

Link to this Internet site from http://www.myreportlinks.com

▶**Miami Museum of Science—Hurricane Main Menu**
Here you can view Hurricane Andrew in 3-D, learn about the hurricane warning system, meet a family who survived Hurricane Andrew, find out which conditions allow a hurricane to exist, and track major hurricanes.

Link to this Internet site from http://www.myreportlinks.com

▶**Ponce de León, Juan**
This site offers a biography of Spanish explorer Juan Ponce de León, who led two expeditions to Florida in the early sixteenth century.

Link to this Internet site from http://www.myreportlinks.com

▶**Ringling Museum of Art**
Here you can take a virtual tour of the John and Mable Ringling Museum of Art, learn about the Ringling Museum of the Circus and Ringling Brothers history, and find out more about the Ringlings' winter residence, Cà d'Zan.

Link to this Internet site from http://www.myreportlinks.com

▶**Smithsonian Journeys: In Search of St. Augustine**
Smithsonian Journeys, a *Smithsonian Magazine* feature, gives you a tour of St. Augustine from its earliest days to the present.

Link to this Internet site from http://www.myreportlinks.com

Report Links

The Internet sites described below can be accessed at
http://www.myreportlinks.com

▶**The Soto Expedition**
Here you can read the epic tale of Spanish explorer Hernando de Soto's ill-fated voyage to Florida. This in-depth article is accompanied by a number of illustrations.

Link to this Internet site from http://www.myreportlinks.com

▶**Stately Knowledge: Florida**
Here you will find basic facts about the state of Florida as well as links to additional online resources about Florida.

Link to this Internet site from http://www.myreportlinks.com

▶**U.S. Census Bureau: Florida**
This Web site features the official census statistics on the state of Florida. Learn about population, demographics, business, geography, and more.

Link to this Internet site from http://www.myreportlinks.com

▶**Welcome to Everglades National Park**
The National Park Service Web site describes the Florida Everglades and Everglades National Park. The "Everglades Ecosystem" section offers information about the region's wildlife, geology, history, and more.

Link to this Internet site from http://www.myreportlinks.com

▶**Welcome to the Florida Citrus Web Site**
Here, at the online home of the Florida Department of Citrus, you can learn all about citrus fruits. The Land for Kids section offers puzzles, games, recipes, and an illustrated guide showing oranges' path from the grove to your glass.

Link to this Internet site from http://www.myreportlinks.com

▶**Zora Neale Hurston (1891–1960)**
This site provides a critical biography of one of the great writers of the Harlem Renaissance, Zora Neale Hurston, who grew up in Florida. Included are an extensive bibliography and a list of Web links.

Link to this Internet site from http://www.myreportlinks.com

Florida Facts

▶ **Capital**
Tallahassee

▶ **Population**
15,982,378*

▶ **Bird**
Mockingbird

▶ **Tree**
Sabal palm

▶ **Flower**
Orange blossom

▶ **Animal**
Florida panther

▶ **Marine Mammal**
Manatee

▶ **Saltwater Mammal**
Dolphin

▶ **Freshwater Fish**
Florida largemouth bass

▶ **Saltwater Fish**
Atlantic sailfish

▶ **Reptile**
Alligator

▶ **Butterfly**
Zebra longwing

▶ **Gem**
Moonstone

▶ **Song**
"Swanee River" (also known as "Old Folks at Home"), words and music by Stephen Foster (1851)

▶ **Motto**
"In God We Trust"

▶ **Nickname**
Sunshine State

▶ **Flag**
Two red bars form an X on the flag's white background. The state seal appears in the middle of the flag, where the bars cross. The state seal of Florida includes a Seminole Indian woman, a sabal palm tree, and a steamboat under the rays of the rising sun, and the words "Great Seal of the State of Florida" and "In God We Trust."

Population reflects the 2000 census.

The State of Florida

Florida is known for warm weather, white sand beaches, Cape Canaveral, and Walt Disney World. But Florida is more than just a magnet for vacationers. The state is also famous for its agriculture—especially its citrus fruit—and is increasingly becoming a national and international business center.

▶ The Sunshine State

Florida is called "the Sunshine State" for good reason. Its warm, sunny weather draws millions of vacationers each year, and the weather is one reason why so many others have made Florida their home. Millions of senior citizens choose the state as a pleasant place for their retirement years. About 18 percent of Floridians are over the age of sixty-five, a greater percentage than in any other state. Florida is the fourth-fastest-growing state in the nation, and the fourth-largest state in terms of population, with nearly 16 million residents in 2000.

The rush to Florida accelerated when George M. Barbour's book *Florida for Tourists, Invalids, and Settlers* was published in 1896. Barbour's description of a tropical paradise proved irresistible: ". . . a settler in Florida— whether he comes as a capitalist, as a farmer, or as a laborer—can live with more ease and personal comfort, can live more cheaply, can enjoy more genuine luxuries, can obtain a greater income from a smaller investment and

▲ *Miami Beach is one of the most famous seaside resorts in the United States.*

by less labor, and can sooner secure a competency, than in any other accessible portion of North America."[1]

The tropical climate allows Floridians and visitors alike to enjoy all sorts of outdoor activities all year long. The beaches are ideal for swimming, snorkeling, scuba diving, windsurfing, and waterskiing. Surfing is popular on some Atlantic beaches. Many visitors enjoy simply looking for seashells. Sanibel Island, on Florida's Gulf Coast, is one of the best places in the world for shelling—each day's high tides wash millions of beautiful new shells onto its beaches. Other popular outdoor activities include golf, fishing, sailing, canoeing, and tennis.

From Far and Wide

Most Floridians come from somewhere else, and about one out of seven were born in another country. This has resulted in a lively and diverse mix of cultures. Many Floridians are from nations in the Caribbean or from Central or South America. About 17 percent of Florida's population (and about half of Miami's population) are Hispanic Americans. Most of them speak Spanish at home. Large groups of Hispanics have come from Colombia, Nicaragua,

▲ *South Beach, part of Miami Beach, features many examples of the Art Deco style, as seen in this photograph of Ocean Drive.*

Guatemala, Honduras, and Peru, but the largest group by far comes from Cuba, which is only ninety miles away from Florida's southern tip.

Refugees and exiles from Cuba make up a neighborhood in Miami known as Little Havana, which is named for the Cuban capital. Little Havana grew quickly after Fidel Castro came to power in Cuba in 1959, and many people decided to leave the island nation. Walk through the streets of Little Havana and you will hear the sounds of salsa music. Spanish is spoken more than English. Within Little Havana are smaller neighborhoods of Hispanic people from other Latin American countries. These neighborhoods include Little Buenos Aires, Little Managua, Little Bogota, Little Quito, and Little Caracas.

About 15 percent of Florida's population is African American. Large groups come from Haiti, Jamaica, and the Bahamas. Haitians are the third-largest group of foreign-born residents in Miami, after Cubans and Canadians, and their neighborhood has come to be known as Little Haiti.

Florida's ethnic mix also includes American Indians. Seminole and Miccosukee Indians live and work in the Everglades area of southern Florida, many on reservations. Other ethnic groups in Florida include Vietnamese, Japanese, and Greeks. There is a large Greek community in Tarpon Springs, where Greek immigrants originally came to dive for sponges.

▶ An Inspiring Atmosphere

Florida's tropical setting has inspired many famous artists, writers, and musicians. Winslow Homer (1836–1910) painted Florida landscapes, and John James Audubon (1785–1851) sketched birds in Key West, at the southern tip of Florida, as part of his *Birds of America* engravings. Today Florida has more art museums than any other state. Among them are the John and Mable Ringling Museum of Art in Sarasota and the Salvador Dalí Museum in St. Petersburg.

Harriet Beecher Stowe (1811–96), who wrote *Uncle Tom's Cabin*, spent winters in Florida. In her book *Palmetto Leaves* she described the scenery of the St. Johns River region. African-American writer Zora Neale Hurston (1903–60) grew up in Eatonville, Florida, and Eatonville is the setting of her novel *Their Eyes Were Watching God.*

Voices From the Gaps: Zora Neale Hurston - Microsoft Internet Explorer

File   Edit   View   Favorites   Tools   Help

Address 🗐 http://voices.cla.umn.edu/authors/ZoraNealeHurston.html   🔗 Go

Biography - Criticism

Though during her life Zora Neale Hurston claimed her birth date as January 7, 1901 and her birth place as Eatonville, Florida, she was actually born on that date in the year 1891 in Notasulga, Alabama. Within the first year or two of her life her family moved to all-black Eatonville, however, and this community shaped her life and her writing to a significant degree. John Hurston, the author's father, was a carpenter and a preacher and was several times elected mayor of their town. Her mother, Lucy, died in 1904. The young Zora didn't take very well to her new stepmother and left home to work for a traveling theatre company, then in 1917 attended Morgan Academy in Baltimore to finish high school. Hurston entered Howard University in 1920 and studied there off and on for the next four years while working as a manicurist to support herself. Her first published story appeared in Howard University's literary magazine in 1921 and she received recognition in 1925 when another story was accepted by the New York magazine **Opportunity**, edited by Charles S. Johnson. After she won second place in the **Opportunity** contest, Johnson and others, including Alain Locke, encouraged Hurston to move to New York.

Zora Neale Hurston

In New York Hurston became part the New Negro movement--later referred to as the Harlem

Done   🌐 Internet

△ *African-American author Zora Neale Hurston grew up in Eatonville, Florida. Many of her works deal with the customs and culture of the southern United States and the Caribbean.*

Marjorie Kinnan Rawlings (1896–1953) won the Pulitzer Prize in 1939 for her novel *The Yearling*. Rawlings lived on a farm in Cross Creek, Florida.

Ernest Hemingway (1899–1961) lived in Key West for ten years. There he wrote *A Farewell to Arms, Death in the Afternoon,* and *To Have and Have Not,* and started work on *For Whom the Bell Tolls.* Pulitzer Prize–winning playwright Tennessee Williams (1911–83), who wrote *The Glass Menagerie, A Streetcar Named Desire,* and *Cat on a Hot Tin Roof,* lived in Key West for thirty-four years. Another writer attracted to Key West was John Hersey (1914–93), whose books include *Key West Tales.*

Miami has become the center of a thriving salsa scene. The city's huge Latino population has provided an enthusiastic audience for many up-and-coming stars of salsa music. Cuban-American singer Gloria Estefan has combined salsa with pop music to appeal to a wide variety of fans.

Land and Climate

Florida is the twenty-second largest state, with a total area of 59,988 square miles. It is bordered on the north by Georgia, on the north and northwest by Alabama, on the east by the Atlantic Ocean, on the south by the Straits of Florida, and on the west by the Gulf of Mexico.

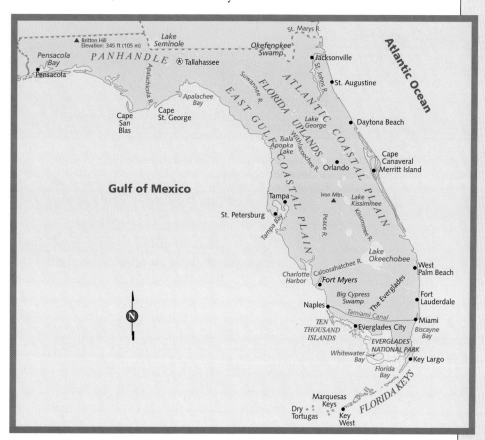

▲ A map of Florida.

▶ Flat as a Pancake

Most of Florida is a huge peninsula, surrounded by water on all sides except the north. The northwestern section of the state is not part of the peninsula, and takes its name, the Panhandle, from its shape—it stretches out like the handle of a frying pan.

The state is nearly as flat as a pancake. There are two vast regions of flat lowlands—the Atlantic Coastal Plain and the East Gulf Coastal Plain. The Atlantic Coastal Plain extends along the state's east coast; the East Gulf Coastal Plain along the west coast and the coast of the Panhandle. Pine forests cover about 50 percent of the lowlands. Wetlands are common. These areas consist of open, grassy marshes and freshwater swamps in which cypress trees grow.

Running up the middle of the Florida peninsula is an area called the Florida Uplands. Despite its name, this is a region of low, rolling hills at an elevation of only 200 to 300 feet above sea level. The Uplands curve around into the northern part of the Panhandle. The highest point in the state—345 feet above sea level—is in Walton County in the Panhandle. No other state has a high point that is so low.

There are more than a thousand miles of sandy beaches along Florida's coasts. No part of Florida is very far from water, either the coastal waters or the thirty thousand lakes and ponds within the state's boundaries. Lake Okeechobee, in the southern part of the state, is Florida's largest lake and the second-largest freshwater lake completely within the United States. There are also several hundred springs, some of which produce healthful mineral waters. Among Florida's many rivers is the Suwannee, featured in Stephen Foster's song "Swanee River" (also

The swamps and marshes that ▶ *make up the Everglades are home to a rich variety of plant and animal life, including this great blue heron.*

called "Old Folks at Home"), which is now Florida's state song. The St. Johns River is Florida's longest.

At the southern tip of the Florida peninsula is Everglades National Park, a huge area of swamps and marshlands. There are wide expanses of sawgrass, a grass with teethlike edges that can grow up to ten feet high. There are tracts of forested land, known as hardwood hammocks, and mangroves, which are trees that grow in salt water along the shoreline. Farther south are the Florida Keys, a chain of three thousand small coral and limestone islands. The Keys stretch from Biscayne Bay National Park near Miami southwestward to the Dry Tortugas, a distance of about 180 miles.

▶ Florida's Wildlife

An enormous variety of plant and animal life is found in Florida. Flowering plants include hibiscus, jacaranda, frangipani, bougainvillea, magnolia, and royal poinciana. Among the many types of palm trees are the sago, coconut, cabbage, royal, and king palm. Trees in many places are draped with ghostlike, tangled Spanish moss that often

American Alligator -- Everglades -- National Wildlife Federation - Microsoft Internet Explorer

File   Edit   View   Favorites   Tools   Help

Address 🔗 http://www.nwf.org/everglades/alligator.html   ▾   𝒞 Go

NATIONAL WILDLIFE FEDERATION®   HOME | CONTACT US | SEARCH

WILDLIFE WORK | EDUCATION | TAKE ACTION | PRINT & FILM | SUPPORT NWF | SHOPPING | GET OUTDOORS | KIDS ZONE

Wetlands

Everglades   why care?

home
why care?
learn more
how to help
NWF efforts

NWF contacts

Join
Free gift
when you
donate online

Lynx Plush Toy

American Alligator

The American alligator is often touted as a species that has made a successful recovery under the Endangered Species Act. In 1967, the U.S. Fish and Wildlife Service listed the alligator as an endangered species throughout its range. Twenty years later, the Service determined that the species had made a full recovery and downlisted it to "threatened due to similarity in appearance" because of its resemblance to the American crocodile. While alligator populations

American alligator. (Photo: Dick Bailey, USFWS)

🔗   🌐 Internet

▲ *Alligators thrive in Florida's swamps.*

forms a canopy overhead. Florida is home to dolphins, sea turtles, manatees, Florida panthers, bald eagles, pelicans, herons, and the world's largest living reptiles—alligators and crocodiles.

Alligators often can be seen taking sunbaths along the banks of rivers and ponds throughout Florida. They can even be found on golf courses. They are usually not dangerous unless they believe their young are in danger or they happen to be very hungry. Humans pose more of a threat to alligators than the other way around. Approximately 10 million Florida alligators died from hunting and draining of their swamp habitat during the first half of the twentieth century. Alligators were classified as an endangered species in the 1940s, and gradually the alligator population began to recover. By 1985, the situation had improved and the alligator's status was changed from "endangered" to "threatened."

Crocodiles are a rare sight in Florida. Still an endangered species, the crocodile is larger and more aggressive than the alligator.

► A Pleasant Climate

For most of the year, Floridians enjoy the pleasant climate for which their state is famous. Miami, in the south, has an average July temperature of 82°F, and Jacksonville in the north has an average July temperature of 81°F. But the summer months can be very hot and humid. Florida's record high temperature of 109°F occurred at Monticello on June 29, 1931.

The yearly average rainfall is 54 inches, most of which (about 32 inches) falls between May and October. On many summer afternoons, a thunderstorm releases a torrential downpour that brings relief from the heat.

Winter temperatures often rise into the 70s on sunny days. Miami has an average January temperature of 67°F, while in Jacksonville the average January temperature is 55°F. Occasionally in winter, a mass of cold air will sweep across northern Florida bringing damaging frost to citrus crops. Cold waves have been known to reach as far south as the Everglades. In 1977, Miami received a light dusting of snow—its first since records started being kept about two centuries ago. Florida's coldest recorded temperature of 2°F occurred at Tallahassee on February 13, 1899.

▶ Hurricane Alley

Throughout its history, Florida has been struck by devastating hurricanes. A hurricane is a tropical cyclone with sustained winds of 74 miles per hour or higher. Some hurricanes in Florida have brought winds of more than 200 miles per hour. Florida's Atlantic Coast is known as Hurricane Alley because it has seen so many ferocious storms. No part of the state, however, is safe from the wrath of hurricanes. They also strike the Gulf Coast frequently and cause flooding and other damage in the interior of the state.

At least one powerful storm hits Florida nearly every year. During hurricane season—usually from August until October or November—all Floridians pay close attention to weather reports. Schoolchildren practice hurricane evacuation. One of the most catastrophic storms to hit Florida was Hurricane Andrew on August 24, 1992. Eighty-five people were killed, thousands were injured, and about a quarter of a million were left homeless. The town of Homestead, just south of Miami, was nearly totally destroyed. Andrew was the country's most expensive natural disaster, causing $25 billion worth of damage.

Economy

Florida is an ideal environment for more than just fun in the sun. It is also an attractive place in which to work or do business. The state's economy is one of the fastest-growing in the nation. Miami, Tampa, Orlando, and Jacksonville have become important financial centers. Miami is also a business gateway to Latin America, and more than 150 multinational corporations have their Latin American head-quarters there.

There are many service and manufacturing industries in Florida. (Service industries provide a variety of business and personal services. They include stores, insurance, real estate, law, and computer software.) High-tech industries, aerospace, agriculture, and commercial fishing are important to the

The Cinderella Castle at Walt ▶ Disney World, in Orlando—one of the most photographed buildings in the world.

state's economy. Abundant sunshine and warm weather give the state a long growing season that is important for agriculture. But Florida's most important industry by far is tourism. At the top of the list of tourist destinations in Florida are Orlando, Miami, Cape Canaveral, and the Florida Keys.

▶ Disney World and Other Parks

Each year, millions of vacationers from all over the world head for the Orlando area, the home of Walt Disney World and numerous other attractions and theme parks. Disney did careful research before choosing Orlando: ". . . beginning in the late 1950s, Walt's staff began looking for a possible location for a second park on the East Coast. Florida seemed likely. Land was cheap and it was warm all year. The coastline was out, though. Walt didn't want to risk hurricanes or people with wet bathing suits visiting his park."[1]

There are twenty major parks in Florida, including SeaWorld and Busch Gardens.

▶ Cape Canaveral

Cape Canaveral on the Atlantic coast, not far from Orlando, is home to the John F. Kennedy Space Center, where visitors can see exhibits presenting the history of the U.S. space program. The main attraction, however, is watching rockets launch into space.

The National Aeronautics and Space Administration (NASA) began operations at Cape Canaveral in 1958 when it launched *Explorer I*, its first earth-orbiting satellite. In 1961, astronaut Alan Shepard took off from Cape Canaveral on a fifteen-minute flight that made him the first American in space. The following year, John Glenn blasted off to become the first U.S. astronaut to orbit the earth. And in 1969, thousands of spectators watched the launch of *Apollo 11*, which carried the first astronauts to land on the moon. Sadly, thousands also saw the disastrous launch of the space shuttle *Challenger* in 1986. All seven astronauts on board were killed when the shuttle exploded shortly after liftoff. But Cape Canaveral still draws huge crowds of visitors eager to see history being made.

▶ Driving Over the Ocean

It is possible to drive over the ocean in Florida. The Overseas Highway (the southernmost stretch of U.S. Highway 1) heads out across the sea for about a hundred miles, all the way to Key West. The Overseas Highway consists mostly of a series of 42 bridges that link the Keys. Writer Joy Williams describes the drive as a dreamlike journey through a watery world: "Everywhere there is water, water that becomes sky, the shadows of rays like clouds moving across the blue. Water

A space shuttle is launched ▶ from NASA's John F. Kennedy Space Center, Cape Canaveral.

loves light. The light changes. Dawn and sunset break. Thunderclouds mass. The water is black, emerald, azure, sheer, and the vault of sky becomes the vault of water."[2]

The Florida Keys are a major tourist destination, with vacation resorts and beaches for swimming, snorkeling, and scuba diving. There are secluded beaches for those who want to be alone, and others with lively crowds for those who prefer company. The Keys are a paradise for those who love to fish, and there are probably some visitors who drive the Overseas Highway just so they can sample genuine Key lime pie at its source. There are three places in the Keys where visitors can swim with dolphins—the Dolphin Research Center, the Theater of the Sea, and Dolphins Plus.

The Overseas Highway ends at Key West, but there are more islands farther out that can be reached by seaplane or boat. About seventy miles southwest of Key West there is a group of seven small islands that make up the Dry Tortugas National Park. *Tortugas* is Spanish for "turtles." There you can visit the ruins of Fort Jefferson, a relic of the Civil War era.

▶ Billions and Billions of Oranges

About 40 billion oranges! That's how many Florida produces each year. The state is famous for its oranges, which are its most important crop. More oranges and grapefruits are grown in Florida than in any other state—about 75 percent of the nation's total. Florida is also the nation's leading producer of tangerines, tangelos, limes, watermelons, and sugarcane. Many other fruits and vegetables are grown in Florida, from tropical fruit such as bananas, papayas, and pineapples to strawberries, tomatoes, avocados, sweet corn, and

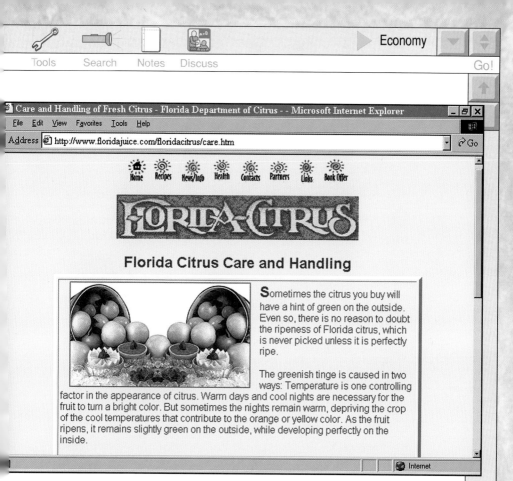

Care and Handling of Fresh Citrus - Florida Department of Citrus - - Microsoft Internet Explorer

File   Edit   View   Favorites   Tools   Help

Address http://www.floridajuice.com/floridacitrus/care.htm   Go

Home   Recipes   News/Info   Health   Contacts   Partners   Links   Book Offer

FLORIDA CITRUS

Florida Citrus Care and Handling

Sometimes the citrus you buy will have a hint of green on the outside. Even so, there is no reason to doubt the ripeness of Florida citrus, which is never picked unless it is perfectly ripe.

The greenish tinge is caused in two ways: Temperature is one controlling factor in the appearance of citrus. Warm days and cool nights are necessary for the fruit to turn a bright color. But sometimes the nights remain warm, depriving the crop of the cool temperatures that contribute to the orange or yellow color. As the fruit ripens, it remains slightly green on the outside, while developing perfectly on the inside.

Internet

▲ *Florida produces about 75 percent of the nation's citrus fruits.*

green peppers. Because of the mild climate, many crops are grown year-round.

More than one third of Florida's land is used for agricultural production. There are approximately forty-five thousand farms in the state, including dairy and beef cattle ranches. Food processing is an important manufacturing industry, the third most important in the state. The main products processed are citrus fruit juices and canned fruits, especially frozen concentrated orange juice, bottled juice, and grapefruit sections.

Chapter 4

Government

On March 3, 1845, the United States Congress admitted Florida to the Union as the twenty-seventh state. Florida's first state constitution was written in 1839, in preparation for statehood.

Florida seceded from the Union on January 10, 1861, and joined the Confederacy. It adopted its second constitution at the same time. When the Civil War ended in 1865, a third constitution was written. A fourth constitution followed in 1868, when Florida reentered the Union, and yet another version was adopted in 1885. The present Florida constitution was adopted in 1969.

Every twenty years, a state commission reviews the constitution. The commission can recommend amendments or changes, or even propose the adoption of an entirely new constitution. The most recent review was in 1998.

In between the twenty-year reviews, state legislators can propose amendments. To become part of the constitution, an amendment must be approved by a three-fifths vote of both houses of the state legislature. Citizens can also propose amendments by presenting a petition signed by a specified number of voters.

▶ The Structure of Florida's Government

Like the federal government, Florida's government is divided into three branches—the executive, legislative, and judicial. The legislative branch creates the laws, the judicial branch interprets the laws, and the executive branch carries out the laws.

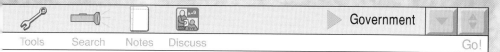

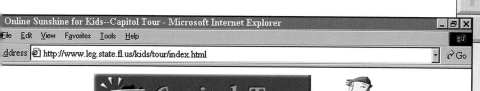

Visit Your
Capitol

[Home] [SiteMap] [Capitol Tour Home]

The Old Capitol

The Capitol has been located in Tallahassee since 1824. The structure today has been restored to its 1902 version, primarily because that is when the dome was added to the building. For many Floridians, the dome is a familiar symbol of state government. The art glass "subdome" allows light into the rotunda.

▲ The Old Capitol building in Tallahassee has been restored to its 1902 version. In 1982, it was reopened as a museum.

Florida's chief executive—the governor—and the lieutenant governor are elected as a team. Voters cast one vote for the two executives. The team is restricted to a maximum of two consecutive four-year terms in office. The governor's cabinet is also part of the executive branch. It includes such officers as the attorney general and the secretary of agriculture.

The legislative branch consists of a 40-member Senate and a 120-member House of Representatives. Floridians vote for senators every four years and for representatives every two years. Senators can serve for two consecutive terms; representatives can serve for four consecutive terms.

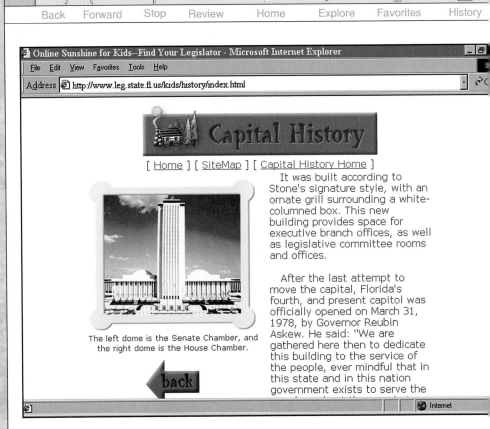

Online Sunshine for Kids--Find Your Legislator - Microsoft Internet Explorer

File   Edit   View   Favorites   Tools   Help

Address   http://www.leg.state.fl.us/kids/history/index.html

Capital History

[Home] [SiteMap] [Capital History Home]

It was built according to Stone's signature style, with an ornate grill surrounding a white-columned box. This new building provides space for executive branch offices, as well as legislative committee rooms and offices.

After the last attempt to move the capital, Florida's fourth, and present capitol was officially opened on March 31, 1978, by Governor Reubin Askew. He said: "We are gathered here then to dedicate this building to the service of the people, ever mindful that in this state and in this nation government exists to serve the

The left dome is the Senate Chamber, and the right dome is the House Chamber.

back

Florida's fourth state capitol building was dedicated in 1978.

When both houses of the legislature approve a bill, it becomes an "act." The governor then has seven working days to either sign or veto the act. If the governor takes no action, the act automatically becomes a law. If the governor vetoes the act, the legislature can override the veto by a two-thirds vote in each house.

The judicial branch of Florida's government consists of the state supreme court, five district courts of appeals, and twenty circuit courts. The governor appoints the seven justices of the state supreme court and the judges of the district courts of appeals to six-year terms. Circuit court judges are elected to six-year terms.

History

During the last Ice Age, much of North America was buried under thick sheets of ice for thousands of years. The sea level was much lower than it is now. A bridge of land joined Siberia and Alaska. About forty thousand years ago, nomadic hunters from Asia began migrating across this

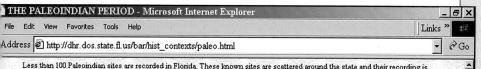

THE PALEOINDIAN PERIOD - Microsoft Internet Explorer

File   Edit   View   Favorites   Tools   Help   Links »

Address http://dhr.dos.state.fl.us/bar/hist_contexts/paleo.html   Go

Less than 100 Paleoindian sites are recorded in Florida. These known sites are scattered around the state and their recording is primarily a result of accidental discoveries. Many more Paleoindian sites undoubtedly exist, but they are located offshore on the continental shelf, in terrestrial wet areas, or are deeply buried. These inaccessible locations make it difficult to identify Paleoindian sites, and our ignorance of them has biased our interpretation of Paleoindian culture.

The Setting

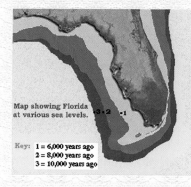

Map showing Florida at various sea levels.

Key: 1 = 6,000 years ago
      2 = 8,000 years ago
      3 = 10,000 years ago

The Paleoindians lived in a Florida twice the size it is today. At the time they lived, sea level was 60-100 m lower, exposing vast expanses of the present continental shelf (Gagliano 1977; Blackwelder et al. 1979). Present-day coasts were inland, even upland, areas. The late Pleistocene shorelines in the Gulf of Mexico were located as much as 120 to 150 km seaward of their present locations. It is not difficult to see why Paleoindian period coastal sites have yet to be discovered in Florida-they are submerged beneath scores of fathoms of ocean water, tens of kilometers offshore (Stright 1986; Garrison 1989).

Pollen and paleontological studies have provided us with evidence of the climate and environment at this time. They indicate that Florida was considerably drier than it is today. Vegetation of north Florida highlands at about 14,000 B.P. generally was open pine forests giving way to oak/hickory stands and local prairies. The central and southern peninsula had open xeric scrub vegetation. Climatic condition of the coasts is still a subject for debate among paleoecologists. The most common view is that

🌐 Internet

▲ Florida's first people, known as Paleo-Indians, inhabited a larger area than exists today. The map above shows lands now covered by water that were once exposed because the sea level was much lower than it is now.

land bridge, following herds of wild animals. By around twelve thousand years ago, various groups of these wandering hunters had spread south and east, and the first groups entered what is now Florida.

▶ Ancient Floridians

The first Floridians, known as Paleo-Indians, were ancestors of today's American Indians. Scientists have discovered stone tools in Florida belonging to the Paleo-Indians. They believe the tools are about twelve thousand years old.

The climate gradually warmed with the ending of the Ice Age. Large animals such as mammoths disappeared, and the Paleo-Indians began hunting smaller animals such as deer and rabbits. Many groups no longer lived a nomadic lifestyle. They were able to find the food they needed closer to their homes. They included more plant foods in their diet. They also discovered the abundant marine life in Florida's rivers, lakes, and bays, and began eating seafood.

By around 1000 B.C., groups of Indians in Florida lived in complex societies based around growing plants. They developed political systems and religious practices. They lived in permanent settlements and built burial mounds, sometimes topped with temples. They produced ceramic bowls and pots, wood carvings, and masks. Clay and stone pipes found where these people once lived suggest that they smoked tobacco. Copper objects found in the area indicate that they traded with groups of Indians as far away as the Great Lakes.

The various Indian tribes in what is now Florida included the Timucua in northern and central Florida, the Calusa in the Tampa Bay area, the Tequesta in southern Florida, the Ais on the Atlantic coast, and the Matecumbe in the Keys. These tribes successfully adapted to their

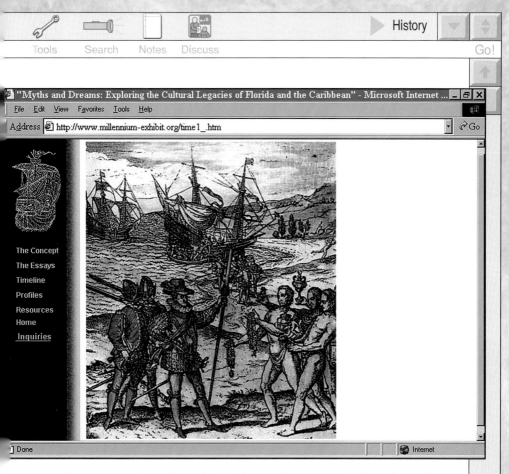

"Myths and Dreams: Exploring the Cultural Legacies of Florida and the Caribbean" - Microsoft Internet ...

File   Edit   View   Favorites   Tools   Help

Address   http://www.millennium-exhibit.org/time1_.htm   Go

The Concept
The Essays
Timeline
Profiles
Resources
Home
Inquiries

▲ *In 1492, Christopher Columbus first made contact with the Indians of
what is now called the West Indies. His voyages to the Americas were
followed by other Spanish expeditions to the Caribbean and Florida.*

environment. They might have thrived in Florida for many
more thousands of years, but the arrival of European
explorers brought many changes.

▶ The Spaniards

Christopher Columbus sailed to the Bahamas on his his-
toric voyage in 1492. There he discovered that the natives
had objects made of gold. On his return to Spain,
Columbus showed some gold trinkets to King Ferdinand
and Queen Isabella. These Spanish rulers were eager for

gold and they gave Columbus ships, soldiers, and weapons for more voyages across the Atlantic.

This search for gold started an era of exploration in the Americas. The Spaniards hoped to find immense treasures in Florida, as they had in Mexico and Peru. They also hoped to convert the natives to Christianity.

On April 2, 1513, Spanish explorer Juan Ponce de León approached the Atlantic shore of what is now Florida. He landed several days later near what is today St. Augustine and claimed the land for Spain. He and his crew had celebrated *Pascua Florida* (Spanish for "the Feast of the

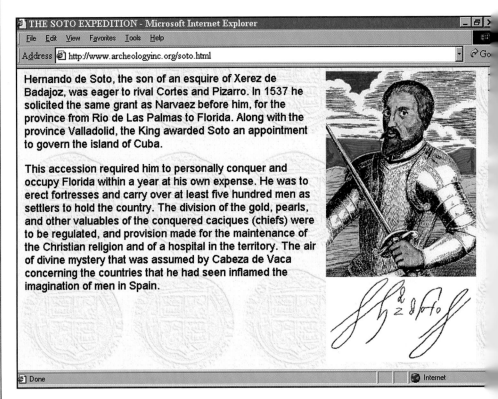

THE SOTO EXPEDITION - Microsoft Internet Explorer

File Edit View Favorites Tools Help

Address http://www.archeologyinc.org/soto.html   Go

Hernando de Soto, the son of an esquire of Xerez de Badajoz, was eager to rival Cortes and Pizarro. In 1537 he solicited the same grant as Narvaez before him, for the province from Rio de Las Palmas to Florida. Along with the province Valladolid, the King awarded Soto an appointment to govern the island of Cuba.

This accession required him to personally conquer and occupy Florida within a year at his own expense. He was to erect fortresses and carry over at least five hundred men as settlers to hold the country. The division of the gold, pearls, and other valuables of the conquered caciques (chiefs) were to be regulated, and provision made for the maintenance of the Christian religion and of a hospital in the territory. The air of divine mystery that was assumed by Cabeza de Vaca concerning the countries that he had seen inflamed the imagination of men in Spain.

Done   Internet

In 1539, Hernando de Soto, a Spanish explorer, landed near what is today Tampa Bay. He led an expedition through Florida in search of gold. Finding none, he traveled west in 1541 to the Mississippi River, the first European explorer to reach it.

Flowers," or Easter), just a few days earlier. So Ponce de León named the new land La Florida. He failed to find gold where he first landed, so he sailed around the southern tip of Florida and up the west coast.

When they went ashore near what is today Tampa, Ponce de León and his party were attacked by the native Calusa Indians. The Spaniards had to retreat. Eight years later, in 1521, Ponce de León returned to the same area. He planned to establish a colony there. But once again the Calusa attacked the Spaniards. Ponce de León was wounded by a poisoned arrow and died a few days later.

Other Spanish explorers followed, still hoping to find gold. In 1528, Pánfilo de Narváez landed near Tampa Bay. He warned the local Indians what would happen to them if they did not obey him and lead him to the gold: "I will take your goods, doing you all the evil and injury that I may be able . . . and I declare to you that the deaths and damages that arise therefrom, will be your fault and not that of His Majesty, nor mine, nor of these cavaliers who came with me."[1] The Indians told Narváez that he would find gold in a land far to the north known as Apalachee. Narváez traveled north as far as Apalachee country, but found no gold. He and most of his men later died in a storm at sea.

In 1539, Hernando de Soto landed in Florida, also near Tampa Bay. De Soto led an expedition through much of Florida, but found no gold.

Despite the lack of treasure, the Spaniards still hoped to colonize the land they claimed in Florida. The French beat them to it. In 1564, Jean Ribaut and a group of French Protestants, known as Huguenots, challenged Spain's claim to the land. They built Fort Caroline on the St. Johns River.

The following year, King Philip II of Spain sent Pedro Menéndez de Avilés to remove the French. Menéndez de Avilés built a fort near the spot where Ponce de León had first landed. It was a short distance south of Fort Caroline. He called his fort San Augustin.

Menéndez de Avilés and his men then marched to Fort Caroline. They destroyed the fort there and killed most of the French settlers. Menéndez de Avilés's fort at San Augustin eventually grew into St. Augustine, the first permanent European settlement in what would become the United States.

Over the next two hundred years, Spain established 140 missions throughout Florida, and the missionaries attempted to convert the native people to Christianity. During this period, the Indian population of Florida began to dwindle. Some died defending their land against the Europeans. Many others died because they had no resistance to the diseases brought by the Europeans, such as chicken pox and measles. Thousands of Indians were captured by European slave traders and taken to islands in the Caribbean.

By 1763, very few of the native people of Florida were still alive. That year, Spain gave Florida to Great Britain as part of the settlement of the Seven Years' War. The Spanish took the last two hundred Indians with them to Cuba when they sailed away from Florida. In less than three hundred years following the voyages of Columbus, the Indian tribes that had inhabited Florida for thousands of years had disappeared.

However, a new Indian people had begun migrating into Florida from Georgia and Alabama. They were the Oconee Creek, and they would later become known as the Seminole.

▷ Florida Changes Hands Again—And Again

The Creek Indians continued to move into Florida during the period of British rule. British settlers established cattle ranches, citrus groves, and sugar and cotton plantations. During the American Revolution (1775–83), many settlers in Georgia and South Carolina who remained loyal to Britain moved to Florida.

But Florida was not a British colony for long. Spain regained control of Florida when the Revolutionary War ended with Britain's withdrawal.

Later, during the War of 1812—which involved the United States, Britain, and France, and lasted until the

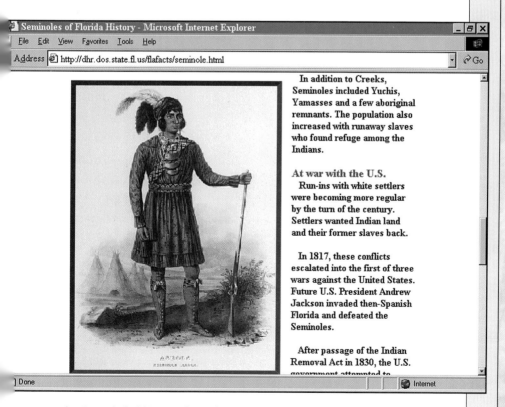

Seminoles of Florida History - Microsoft Internet Explorer

File   Edit   View   Favorites   Tools   Help

Address ☐ http://dhr.dos.state.fl.us/flafacts/seminole.html

In addition to Creeks, Seminoles included Yuchis, Yamasses and a few aboriginal remnants. The population also increased with runaway slaves who found refuge among the Indians.

At war with the U.S.
Run-ins with white settlers were becoming more regular by the turn of the century. Settlers wanted Indian land and their former slaves back.

In 1817, these conflicts escalated into the first of three wars against the United States. Future U.S. President Andrew Jackson invaded then-Spanish Florida and defeated the Seminoles.

After passage of the Indian Removal Act in 1830, the U.S. government attempted to

Done   ● Internet

▲ Osceola led his people in the First and Second Seminole Wars, until his capture in 1837.

end of 1814—Spain allowed Britain to use Pensacola as a naval base. In 1819, with the signing of the Adams-Onís Treaty, the United States acquired Florida from Spain. In 1822, it officially became the Territory of Florida.

Meanwhile, conflict had developed in Florida between European settlers and Indians. Settlers moving in often forced the Indians out. In 1823, Florida officials decided to locate the new capital midway between St. Augustine and Pensacola. They chose a village of Talasi Indians as their site. They chased the Indians away, and Tallahassee was established.

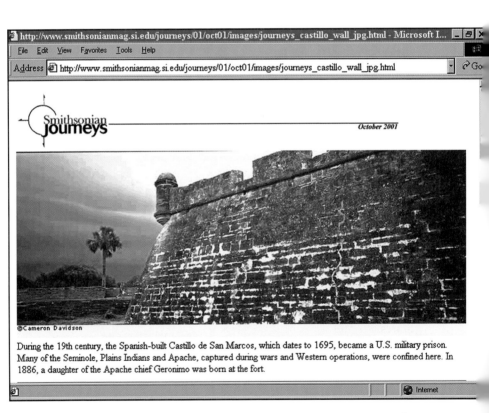

http://www.smithsonianmag.si.edu/journeys/01/oct01/images/journeys_castillo_wall_jpg.html - Microsoft I...

File   Edit   View   Favorites   Tools   Help

Address   http://www.smithsonianmag.si.edu/journeys/01/oct01/images/journeys_castillo_wall_jpg.html   Go

Smithsonian journeys   October 2001

©Cameron Davidson

During the 19th century, the Spanish-built Castillo de San Marcos, which dates to 1695, became a U.S. military prison. Many of the Seminole, Plains Indians and Apache, captured during wars and Western operations, were confined here. In 1886, a daughter of the Apache chief Geronimo was born at the fort.

Internet

▲ Castillo de San Marcos, in St. Augustine, is the oldest masonry fort in the continental United States. Construction was begun on the fort in 1672.

The Indians who were driven from their lands had fled to the forests. They became known as *Se-mi-no-lee*, a Creek word meaning "wild ones" or "runaways." The attempts by the U.S. government to remove the Seminole from their lands resulted in three Seminole wars. In the First Seminole War (1817–18), the Indians were led by Osceola, the son of an Indian woman and a European settler. The Seminole were defeated by General Andrew Jackson in the first war. Osceola was captured in 1837 during the Second Seminole War (1835–42). He died of malaria the following year. The Second Seminole War also ended in defeat for the Indians. The Third Seminole War (1855–58) was their final effort. Most of the Seminole were killed in that war. During it, a Seminole leader known as Coacoochee told his people, "The white men are as thick as the leaves in the hammock; they come upon us thicker every year. They may shoot us, drive our women and children night and day; they may chain our hands and feet, but the red man's heart will always be free."[2] Several hundred Seminole managed to escape to the Everglades, where they survived in freedom.

Statehood Then Secession

Florida joined the Union in 1845. One of Florida's first two senators was David Levy Yulee, who served from 1845 to 1851. He was the first Jewish member of the United States Senate.

Florida would not remain in the Union for long, however. About half of the population of Florida was made up of slaves working on plantations. The economic well-being of Florida's plantation owners depended on slave labor. With the antislavery Republican Party in charge in Washington, D.C., the slaveholders feared that their way

of life was threatened. On January 10, 1861, Florida became the third state to secede from the Union in order to side with the Confederacy.

The Civil War (1861–65) proved to be a disaster for Florida and the rest of the Confederacy. At least five thousand Floridians died, and many cities and plantations were left in ruins. The economy was in shambles. Florida's slaves were freed, but they would face a century of discrimination and segregation.

Gradually, however, Florida recovered from the war. Northerners were drawn to Florida by the opportunity to

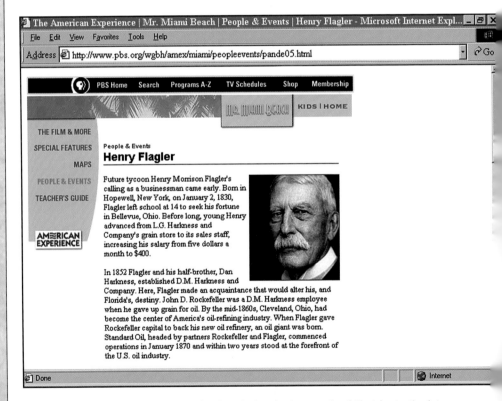

The American Experience | Mr. Miami Beach | People & Events | Henry Flagler - Microsoft Internet Expl...

File   Edit   View   Favorites   Tools   Help

Address http://www.pbs.org/wgbh/amex/miami/peopleevents/pande05.html   Go

PBS Home   Search   Programs A-Z   TV Schedules   Shop   Membership

KIDS I HOME

THE FILM & MORE
SPECIAL FEATURES
MAPS
PEOPLE & EVENTS
TEACHER'S GUIDE

AMERICAN
EXPERIENCE

People & Events
Henry Flagler

Future tycoon Henry Morrison Flagler's calling as a businessman came early. Born in Hopewell, New York, on January 2, 1830, Flagler left school at 14 to seek his fortune in Bellevue, Ohio. Before long, young Henry advanced from L.G. Harkness and Company's grain store to its sales staff, increasing his salary from five dollars a month to $400.

In 1852 Flagler and his half-brother, Dan Harkness, established D.M. Harkness and Company. Here, Flagler made an acquaintance that would alter his, and Florida's, destiny. John D. Rockefeller was a D.M. Harkness employee when he gave up grain for oil. By the mid-1860s, Cleveland, Ohio, had become the center of America's oil-refining industry. When Flagler gave Rockefeller capital to back his new oil refinery, an oil giant was born. Standard Oil, headed by partners Rockefeller and Flagler, commenced operations in January 1870 and within two years stood at the forefront of the U.S. oil industry.

Done   Internet

▲ Henry Flagler is credited with developing much of Florida. In the late nineteenth and early twentieth centuries, he helped organize what became the Florida East Coast Railroad.

own land—new settlers were given 160-acre parcels of land for homesteading. By 1880, Florida's population had doubled to about 270,000.

The Coming of the Railroads—And More and More People

Henry Morrison Flagler (1830–1913), a very wealthy man, founded the Standard Oil Company with John D. Rockefeller. He was determined to speed up the development of Florida. He envisioned a string of hotels along the Atlantic coast. A railroad would be built to link them and would bring vacationers from the North.

During the 1880s, Flagler built his first hotel in St. Augustine. By 1896, he had built many others. He also had completed his Florida East Coast Railway, which ran down the coast to Miami. Next, he built a railway all the way to Key West by constructing a series of bridges in the Keys. But he didn't stop there—he also provided steamships to carry people from Key West to Cuba.

Meanwhile, Henry B. Plant (1819–99) had built the Plant Railroad System. It ran along Florida's Gulf Coast and also linked Tampa to Jacksonville. It made the shipment of goods much easier. Before long, Florida was booming. The population grew further after 1898 as U.S. troops settled in Florida after serving in the Spanish-American War.

During the early years of the twentieth century, wealthy people who vacationed in Florida built elaborate estates there. Land was reclaimed, making new areas available for housing. Canals were built to deliver water. World War I provided further fuel to the booming economy. New communities sprang up almost overnight. Roads were built, and soon tourists were arriving in Florida by car.

▲ *The Overseas Highway connects the islands of the Florida Keys to the mainland.*

Carl Fisher (1874–1939) was a man who had made his fortune in the automobile industry. He dredged sand from the bottom of Biscayne Bay to create Miami Beach. Development quickly followed. Soon, what had been a tangled mass of mangroves off the shore of Miami became a fancy resort. In 1925 alone, 481 hotels and apartment houses were built there.

▶ A Series of Disasters

In 1926, a devastating hurricane turned the land boom into a land bust. The hurricane killed at least four hundred people and injured thousands. Homes, businesses, and other buildings were destroyed. People realized that it was risky to own property in areas vulnerable to hurricanes. Property values plunged and this caused many banks to fail.

There was another deadly hurricane in 1928. Then came the 1929 stock market crash and the Great Depression of the 1930s. On September 2, 1935, a disastrous hurricane struck the Florida Keys. Flagler's railroad bridges were destroyed, and more than four hundred lives were lost.

▲ *Tourism is Florida's most important industry. The Boca Raton Resort & Club, located in Florida's fabled Palm Beach County, is world-renowned.*

The Overseas Highway, completed in 1938, replaced the railroad to the Keys. Florida's economy finally recovered during America's participation in World War II (1941–45).

Promise and Challenge

During the second half of the twentieth century, Florida's continued growth and prosperity surpassed the wildest dreams of its early promoters.

Tourism and agriculture were both important to the booming economy: "At midcentury tourism held a slight lead over agriculture as the state's leading revenue producer. Taking full advantage of Florida's geographical location, its sunshine and climate, miles of wide beaches, interior scenic attractions, and popularly priced automobiles, the travel and recreation industries enjoyed what has been called the 1950 boom. Almost a million automobiles crossed into Florida that year for recreational purposes."[3]

The World of Disney and Other Attractions

Tourism increased dramatically again in the 1970s with the opening of Walt Disney World in Orlando. The "Space Coast" at Cape Canaveral also drew tourists. Space-related high-tech industries were developed. The influx of Cuban refugees after 1959 contributed to Miami's importance as a center of commerce and culture. And the rebirth of Miami Beach's Art Deco district transformed the city into a fashion and glamour capital. Florida's other cities grew and prospered.

The Price of Growth

Florida's growth has come at a price. Development near the Everglades threatens the region's natural beauty and wildlife. Dikes and canals built early in the twentieth century reclaimed land for farming and housing, but the natural flow of water from Lake Okeechobee through the Everglades was restricted. Now the Everglades becomes parched during years of drought. During wet years the Everglades is contaminated by chemicals and fertilizers that seep into the water from farms.

Floridians hope to save the Everglades. An ambitious ecosystem recovery project has been proposed. It involves the creation of a huge underground water-storage system, at a cost of billions of dollars. Floridians are determined to protect their Sunshine State.

▲ Floridians are determined to protect one of their greatest natural treasures, the Everglades, from pollution and development.

Chapter Notes

Chapter 1. The State of Florida

1. George M. Barbour, *Florida for Tourists, Invalids, and Settlers*, 1896, quoted in Paul Zach, ed., *Florida*, Third Edition (Hong Kong: Apa Productions, Ltd., 1984), p. 49.

Chapter 3. Economy

1. Katherine Greene and Richard Greene, *The Man Behind the Magic: The Story of Walt Disney* (New York: Viking, 1991), p. 155.

2. Joy Williams, *The Florida Keys* (New York: Random House, 1987), p. 59.

Chapter 5. History

1. Paul Zach, ed., *Florida*, Third Edition (Hong Kong: Apa Productions, Ltd., 1984), p. 27.

2. Ibid., p. 38.

3. Michael Gannon, *Florida: A Short History* (Gainesville: University Press of Florida, 1993), p. 3.

Further Reading

Anderson, Peter. *John James Audubon: Wildlife Artist.* New York: Franklin Watts, 1995.

De Hart, Allen. *Adventuring in Florida.* San Francisco: Sierra Club Books, 1991.

Downs, Sandra. *Florida in the Civil War: A State in Turmoil.* Brookfield, Conn.: Twenty-First Century Books, Inc., 2001.

Fradin, Dennis Brindell. *Florida.* Danbury, Conn.: Children's Press, 1994.

Heinrichs, Ann. *Florida.* Danbury, Conn.: Children's Press, 1998.

Hurston, Zora Neale. *Their Eyes Were Watching God.* New York: HarperCollins, 1999.

Jenkins, Peter. *Along the Edge of America.* Nashville: Rutledge Hill Press, 1995.

Leslie, Candace. *Hidden Florida Keys and Everglades.* Berkeley, Calif.: Ulysses Press, 1990.

Rawlings, Marjorie Kinnan. *The Yearling.* New York: Atheneum Books for Young Readers, 1985.

Selby, Nick and Corinna Selby. *Florida.* Oakland, Calif.: Lonely Planet Publications, 1997.

Weitzel, Kelley G. *The Timucua: A Native American Detective Story.* Gainesville: University Press of Florida, 2000.

Index